Ultimate WEDDING SHOWSTOPPERS

KT-194-491

Project Managers: Carol Cuellar and Zobeida Pérez
Art Design: Ken Rehm
Text By: Fucini Productions, Inc.
Special thanks to David, Larry, Gail, Vincent, Mike, and Ken for their creative input

CONTENTS

Ultimate WEDDING SHOWSTOPPERS

Introduction

Journey back with us to a wedding in ancient Rome. How incredibly familiar this ceremony from a long-vanished civilization is to our modern eyes! There, in their flowing gowns, as beautiful and lovely as flowers in a field, are the bridesmaids. A nervous groom stands next to a veiled bride. Under the watchful and tender gaze of family and friends, the two exchange vows, ever-so-gently slip rings on one another's fingers, and seal their bond with a kiss. Later, there will be a ceremonial wedding cake, an early predecessor of the layered confections cut by brides and grooms today.

How fitting it is that the wedding ceremony has retained so many of its traditions from century to century and even from civilization to civilization.

After all, what is more enduring than the love that brings a bride and groom together on their wedding day? Empires may rise and fall, technology may overthrow old ideas about time and space, and our culture may bear little resemblance to the world our grandparents knew. But people will always regard their wedding as one of the most special days of their lives. It was that way in the ancient world, and it will remain so two thousand years from now.

Weddings are as enduring as love, which means they will be with us for as long as our human hearts beat. The Romans recognized this by exchanging iron wedding rings. Iron was chosen because its great strength represented the permanence of the marriage bond. But the symbolism of the ring's *shape* was even more significant to ancient lovers, just as it is to lovers today.

There are no parts to a circular ring—it is simply one. Nor does a ring have an end—its circle is complete and eternal, never stopping, never breaking. Are not these the qualities a bride and groom seek on their wedding day, when two become one in a union that lasts for eternity?

Music: The Language of Love

Like the wedding ring, music celebrates and symbolizes the union that a bride and groom enter on this special day. That's why song and dance were a part of the wedding ceremony long before the ancient Romans built their great city. Music has always occupied a unique place in weddings, just as it has in the lives of lovers.

It is music that gives voice to those mysterious feelings that must be expressed but can never be captured in mere words. "I love you more than I can say." How many times have star-struck lovers whispered this declaration? Isn't this why every romantic relationship seems to be punctuated by music? *This is the song that was playing when I first saw you.* "This is the song we used to listen to when we dated." "Remember when we sang along to this song during that trip through the mountains?"

Music is woven into the fabric of every relationship. We hear our love echo in its rich melodies and feel our hearts draw closer as its harmonies sweep us away. No wonder the practice of selecting a special "wedding song" has become a cherished tradition among lovers everywhere.

During the wedding ceremony, the band will play this special song, and with all eyes on them, the couple will step onto the dance floor. As we watch and listen, we will learn much about this newly married couple and the bond that joins them with the unwavering strength of an ancient Roman iron. They cannot describe this bond in words, for it defies verbal descriptions. To understand it, we must listen to their song.

The Wedding Songs

Love takes many shapes and forms, so it is only fitting that lovers have selected such a great variety of wedding songs, from the whimsical "Love and Marriage" to the philosophical "Wedding Song (There Is Love)" to the passionate "In Your Eyes." Yet, despite their rich diversity, great wedding songs share a common theme—celebration of the total, complete, and unending dedication that true lovers have for one another.

This sentiment is expressed beautifully in one of our most beloved wedding songs, the aptly titled "All the Way." Written by the team of Sammy Cahn and Jimmy Van Heusen, this song, which was performed by Frank Sinatra in the film *The Joker Is Wild*, won an Oscar in 1957. In simple yet elegant terms, the song reminds us of an eternal truth: *Love is never a part-time proposition.* It is not a feeling that can be trotted out only at convenient or opportune moments. For, as Sammy Cahn's lyrics admonish, "When somebody loves you / It's no good unless he loves you—all the way."

Delivered in Sinatra's smooth, melodious style, "All the Way" touched the hearts of lovers everywhere. A generation later, another popular love song from a hit film had a similar effect on young couples. Lionel Richie wrote the words and music for "Endless Love" at the request of film director Franco Zeffirelli, who wanted a theme song for the movie he was making, starring Brooke Shields and Martin Hewitt as the doomed teenage lovers Jade and David. The film (also entitled *Endless Love*) and the Richie song both became major hits in 1981 because they beautifully celebrated the power of love to overcome all obstacles and justify any sacrifice.

Richie recorded "Endless Love" as a duet with Diana Ross during an early-morning studio session in Lake Tahoe, Nevada. The song reached the top of the charts in August and remained there for nine weeks. More than two million copies of the song were sold, establishing a record for sales of a duet. A popular wedding song throughout the world, "Endless Love" was nominated for two Grammys and an Oscar. The song also won a People's Choice Award.

In addition to paying homage to the eternal union between two people, some wedding songs celebrate the power of love to transform those who experience its magic. Among the most moving songs in this category is "Best Thing That Ever Happened to Me."

Written by Mississippi-born country/R&B composer and artist Jim Weatherly, the song became a smash hit in 1973 for Gladys Knight & The Pips. Anyone who has ever had their life changed by someone special can't help but be moved by Weatherly's unforgettable lines:

> **If anyone should ever write my life story**
> **For what ever reason there might be**
> **Oh, you'll be there between each line of pain and glory**
> **'Cause you're the best thing that ever happened to me.**

As was the case with "All the Way" and "Endless Love," hit films have often been the source of our most popular wedding songs. This should come as no surprise. Cinema, after all, shares much in common with a wedding ceremony: color, pageantry, human drama, and romance. And isn't going to the movies one of the most popular dates among young couples?

In keeping with the universal appeal of wedding songs, many of these romantic film tunes have become major hits. "Up Where We Belong," the sweet, raspy duet performed by Joe Cocker and Jennifer Warnes from the film *An Officer and a Gentleman*, was No. 1 on the *Billboard* charts. The Bryan Adams hit "(Everything I Do) I Do It for You" from the film *Robin Hood: Prince of Thieves* topped the *Billboard* charts for seven straight weeks and earned a Grammy Award. The song became the longest-running No. 1 single in the history of the United Kingdom, remaining on its exalted perch for 16 straight weeks. This hauntingly beautiful song reminds us that giving of oneself completely is at the essence of true love. In so doing, the song reaffirms the commitment of couples on their wedding day.

Some love songs seem to fit so perfectly into the romantic theme of a film that their emergence as wedding-ceremony classics seems almost assured. Such was the case with "Where Do I Begin," the theme song from the romantic movie *Love Story*, starring Ali McGraw and Ryan O'Neal as the two ill-fated lovers Jenny and Oliver. Capturing the tragic romance of the film, this song, written by former New York attorney Carl Sigman and Francis Lai, won an Oscar and sold more than six million copies.

The Wedding March

Today, young couples are influenced by movies when selecting their wedding songs. Years ago, before the birth of cinema, royalty held sway over the choice of wedding music. Felix Mendelssohn's famous composition "The Wedding March" became a fixture at nuptial ceremonies nine years after the great composer's death, when Victoria, Princess of Great Britain, selected it for her own 1858 wedding to Prince Frederick William of Prussia.

Taken from Mendelssohn's *A Midsummer Night's Dream,* the jubilant and triumphant passage captured the bright, shining promise of a wedding ceremony. Inspired by Britain's charming princess, brides throughout Europe began insisting that the piece be played at their weddings. By the 1870s, the music, which had become known as "The Wedding March," or more simply "Here Comes the Bride," was established as a custom in the United States as well.

Mendelssohn composed the overture to *A Midsummer Night's Dream* when he was only 17. Another 17 years would pass before he would write the incidental music to this composition, including "The Wedding March." The great romantic composer died a short time later when he was only 38. Today, "The Wedding March" is undoubtedly Mendelssohn's most famous composition. Indeed, there are few people in the industrialized world who do not instantly recognize the opening to this inspirational piece.

The sweeping popularity of "The Wedding March" shows that music, like true love, has the power to transcend time and place. So go ahead and enjoy our banquet of great wedding songs. After all, what better way is there to celebrate the universal tradition of the wedding ceremony than with the *universal language* of music? You might say that the two share a marriage made in heaven.

The Whos, Whats, and Whys of Weddings

1. The custom of tying old shoes to the back of the bridal car grew out of a tradition begun in Tudor England. It seems that wedding guests of the era threw shoes at the wedding carriage. Hitting the carriage was said to bring good luck to the newlyweds.

2. The custom of wearing a white wedding gown was started in 1499 by Anne of Brittany, when she married Louis XII of France.

3. In Fiji, it is customary for the groom to present the bride's father with a whale's tooth.

4. Rain on your wedding day is considered a sign of good luck in India.

5. In Jewish wedding ceremonies, the groom breaks a glass to symbolize the destruction of the Temple in Jerusalem. Among Greeks, breaking plates at a wedding reception is thought to bring good luck.

6. Greek tradition calls for rolling the babies of friends and family members on the matrimonial bed to ensure that the newlyweds will have children.

7. During traditional Chinese wedding ceremonies, the couple drinks wine and honey from goblets tied together by red string. Red is chosen to symbolize love.

8. At many Swedish weddings, the bride wears a silver coin from her father in her left shoe and a gold coin from her mother in her right.

FROM THIS MOMENT ON

Words and Music by
SHANIA TWAIN and R.J. LANGE

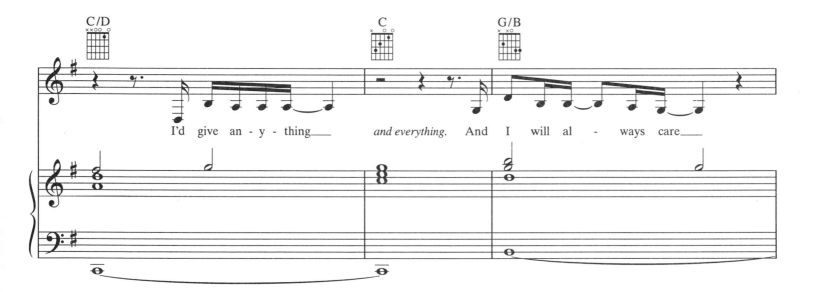

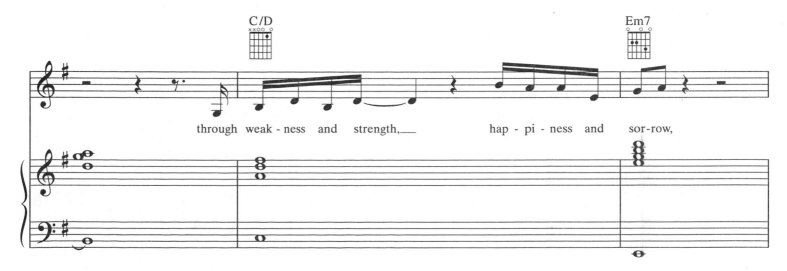

From This Moment On - 7 - 1

WEDDING SONG
(There Is Love)

THIS I PROMISE YOU

Words and Music by
RICHARD MARX

IT HAD TO BE YOU

Words by
GUS KAHN

Music by
ISHAM JONES

BECAUSE YOU LOVED ME
(Theme from "Up Close & Personal")

Words and Music by
DIANE WARREN

love I found_ in you,_ I'll be for - ev - er thank - ful, ba - by.
love, I had_ it all._ I'm grate - ful for_ each day_ you gave_ me.

You're the one_ who held_ me up, nev - er let_ me fall._
May - be I_ don't know_ that much, but I know this much_ is true._

You're the one_ who saw_ me through, through it all._ } You were_ my
I was blessed_ be - cause_ I was loved by you._

Chorus:

strength when I_ was weak, you were_ my voice when I could - n't speak. You were_ my

Lyrics:
voice when I could-n't speak. You were_ my eyes when I could-n't see, you saw_ the
best there was_ in me, lift-ed_ me_ up when I could-n't reach. You gave_ me
faith 'coz you_ be-lieved._ I'm ev-ery-thing_ I am be-cause_ you
loved_ me. I'm ev-ery-thing_ I am be-cause_ you loved_ me.

AMAZED

Tune guitar down a half step

Slowly ♩ = 76

Words and Music by
MARV GREEN, AIMEE MAYO
and CHRIS LINDSEY

Ev-'ry lit-tle thing that you do,___ ba-by, I'm a-mazed by___ you.

Ev-'ry lit-tle thing that you do,_____ I'm so in love___ with you.

_____ It just keeps get-ting bet - ter.

Verse 2:
The smell of your skin,
The taste of your kiss,
The way you whisper in the dark.
Your hair all around me,
Baby, you surround me;
You touch every place in my heart.
Oh, it feels like the first time every time.
I wanna spend the whole night in your eyes.
(To Chorus:)

LET IT BE ME
(Je T'appartiens)

Music by GILBERT BECAUD
English Words by MANN CURTIS
French Words by PIERRE DELANOE

TONIGHT I CELEBRATE MY LOVE

Words and Music by
MICHAEL MASSER and GERRY GOFFIN

Slowly and Expressively ♩ = 60

1..To-

Verse:

night   I cel - e - brate my love _____ for you;   it
night   I cel - e - brate my love _____ for you;   and
3.(See additional lyrics)

seems   the nat - u - ral   thing _____ to do.   To -
hope   that deep in - side you   feel _____ it too.   To -

Tonight I Celebrate My Love - 4 - 1

Chorus:

Verse 3:
Tonight I celebrate my love for you,
And soon this old world will seem brand new.
Tonight we will both discover
How friends turn into lovers,
When I make love to you.
(To Chorus:)

From the Paramount Picture "THE JOKER IS WILD"

ALL THE WAY

Lyric by
SAMMY CAHN

Music by
JAMES VAN HEUSEN

ALWAYS

Written by
JONATHAN LEWIS, WAYNE LEWIS
and DAVID LEWIS

Always - 3 - 1

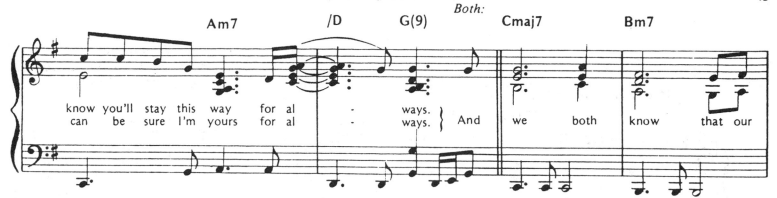

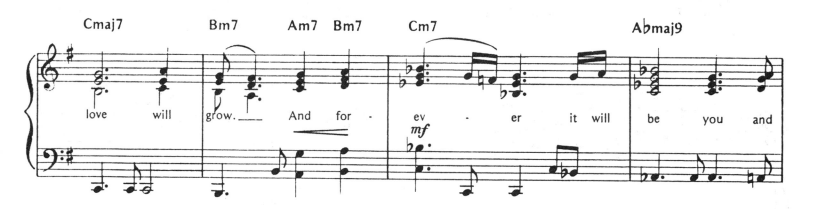

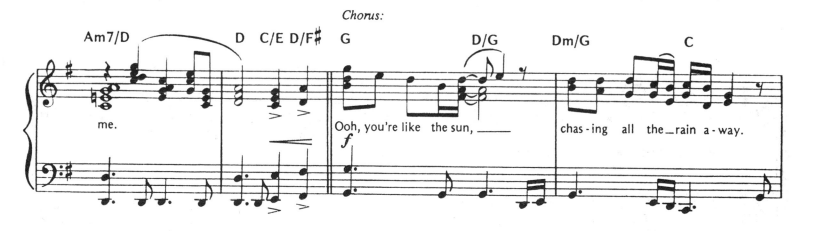

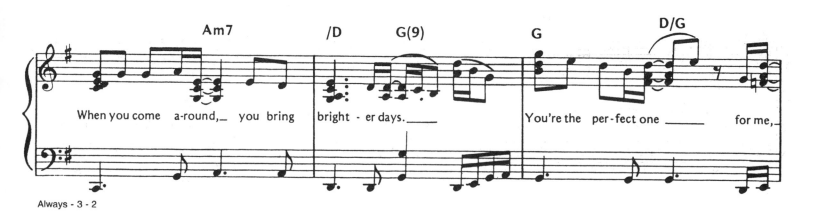

Always - 3 - 2

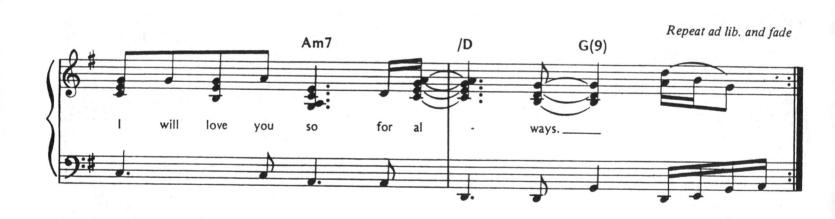

From the United Artists Motion Picture "THE HAPPY ENDING"

WHAT ARE YOU DOING THE REST OF YOUR LIFE?

Lyrics by
ALAN and
MARILYN BERGMAN

Music by
MICHEL LEGRAND

What Are You Doing the Rest of Your Life? - 3 - 1

48

WHEN I FALL IN LOVE

Words by
EDWARD HEYMAN

Music by
VICTOR YOUNG

I CROSS MY HEART

Words and Music by
STEVE DORFF and ERIC KAZ

I Cross My Heart - 5 - 1

58

Additional Lyrics

2. You will always be the miracle
   That makes my life complete.
   And as long as there's a breath in me
   I'll make yours just as sweet.
   As we look into the future,
   It's as far as we can see.
   So let's make each tomorrow
   Be the best that it can be.
   (To Chorus)

From the Motion Picture "THE MIRROR HAS TWO FACES"

I FINALLY FOUND SOMEONE

Words and Music by
BARBRA STREISAND, MARVIN HAMLISCH,
R.J. LANGE and BRYAN ADAMS

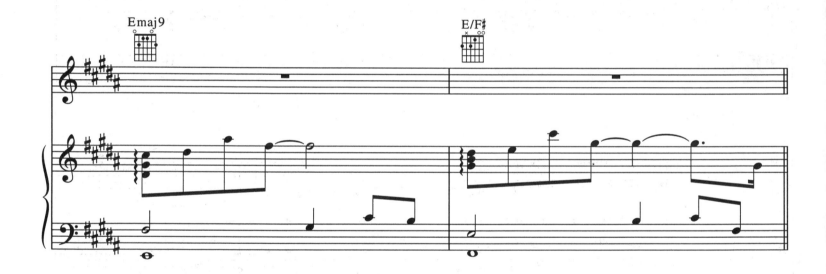

I Finally Found Someone - 8 - 1

I SWEAR

Words and Music by
GARY BAKER and FRANK MYERS

Additional lyrics

2. I'll give you everything I can,
    I'll build your dreams with these two hands,
    And we'll hang some memories on the wall.
    And when there's silver in your hair,
    You won't have to ask if I still care,
    'Cause as time turns the page my love won't age at all.
    (To Chorus)

LOVE AND MARRIAGE

Lyric by
SAMMY CAHN

Music by
JAMES VAN HEUSEN

Love and Marriage - 2 - 1

From the Twentieth Century Fox Motion Picture "ONE FINE DAY"

FOR THE FIRST TIME

Words and Music by
JAMES NEWTON HOWARD,
ALLAN RICH and JUD FRIEDMAN

Slowly ♩ = 62

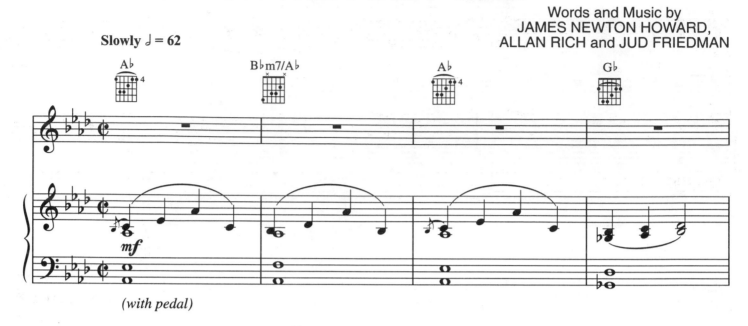

(with pedal)

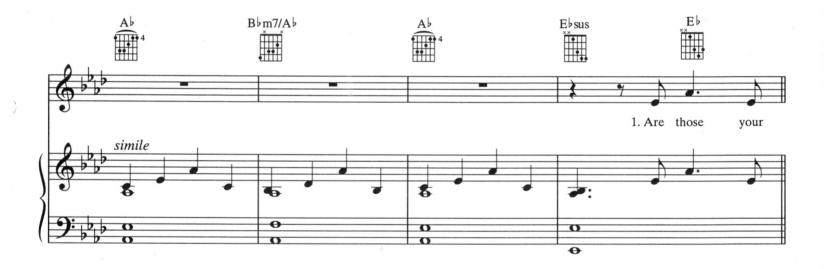

1. Are those your

Verse:

eyes?   Is____ that your smile?   I've been
real?   Can____ this be true?   Am I the

For the First Time - 6 - 1

Now I un-der-stand___ what_____ love___ is,

love__ is for the first time.____

FROM HERE TO ETERNITY

Words and Music by
MICHAEL PETERSON and
ROBERT ELLIS ORRALL

From Here to Eternity - 3 - 1

2. Well, I saved a

I prom - ise__ my love to you, I'm will - ing and a - ble and read -

y to...__ what - ev - er you need,__ I am here__ for you.__ And

I'll al - ways be,__ from here to e - ter - ni - ty.

Verse 2:
Well, I saved a year for this ring,
I can't wait to see how it looks on your hand.
I'll give you everything that one woman needs
From a one-woman man.
I'll be strong, I'll be tender, a man of my word.
And I will be yours...
(To Chorus:)

From the Tri-Star Pictures Film " Chances Are"

AFTER ALL

(Love Theme from "Chances Are")

Music by
DEAN PITCHFORD
and TOM SNOW

After All - 5 - 1

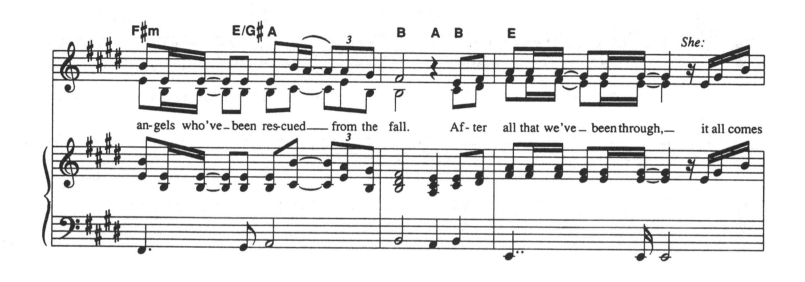

After All - 5 - 3

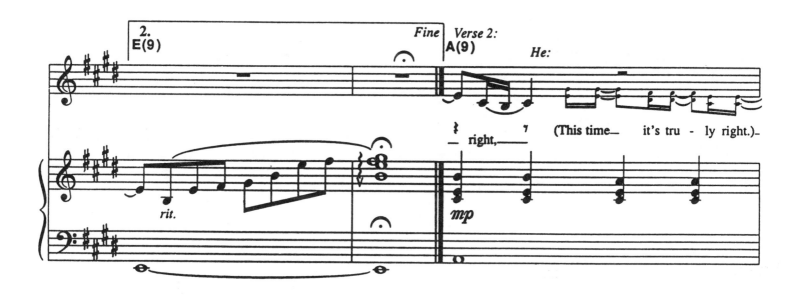

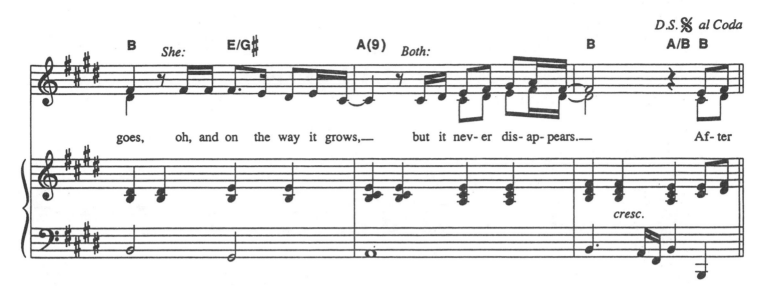

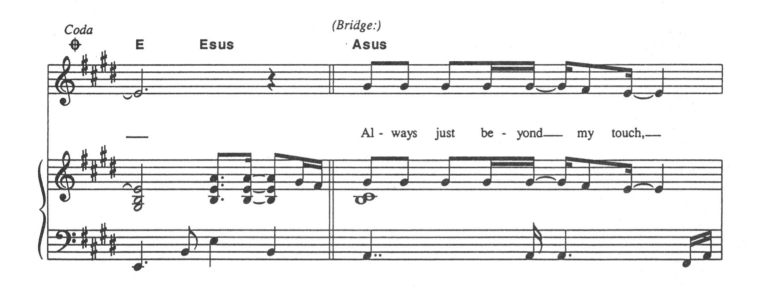

From the Original Motion Picture Soundtrack "THE THREE MUSKETEERS"

ALL FOR LOVE

Written by
BRYAN ADAMS, ROBERT JOHN "MUTT" LANGE
and MICHAEL KAMEN

All for Love - 6 - 1

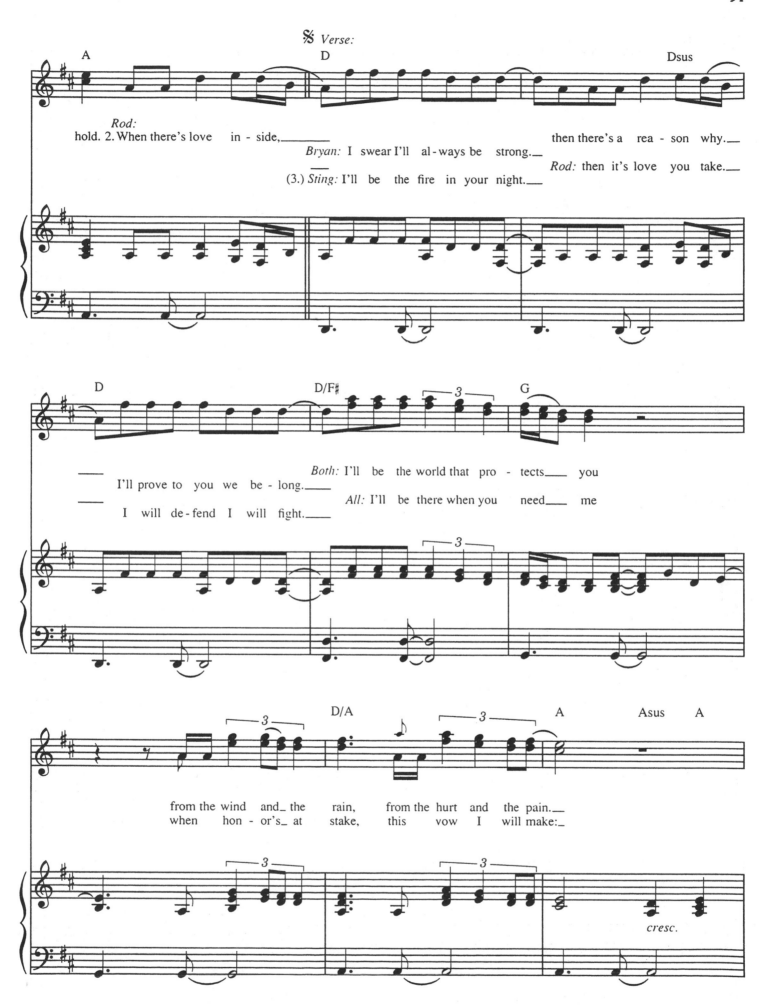

92

94

All for Love - 6 - 5

ALL I HAVE

Words and Music by
BETH NIELSEN CHAPMAN
and ERIC KAZ

Moderately slow ♩ = 72

mp

(with pedal)

Verse:

1. You can say   you love__ me,
(2.) feel like I've known___ you for - ev - er___ and ev - er, ba - by, that's___ how close___ we are.__

and I   be - lieve___ that's   true.__

Chorus:

ALL I EVER NEED IS YOU

Words and Music by
JIMMY HOLIDAY and
EDDIE REEVES

Moderately

Some - times when I'm down and all a - lone, just like a child with-out a home. The love you give me keeps me hang-in' on Oh hon - ey, All I Ev - er Need Is You. You're my first love, you're my last, You're my fu - ture, you're my past.

And lov-ing you is all I ask, Hon-ey, All I Ev-er Need Is You.

Win-ters come and they go, and we watch the melt-ing

snow. Sure as sum-mer fol-lows spring, all the things you do

give me a rea-son to build my world a-round you. Some men fol-low rain-bows, I am

ALL MY LIFE

Words and Music by
RORY BENNETT and
JO JO HAILEY

All My Life - 7 - 1

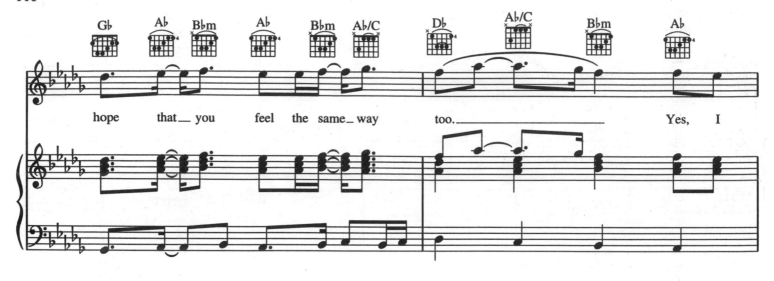

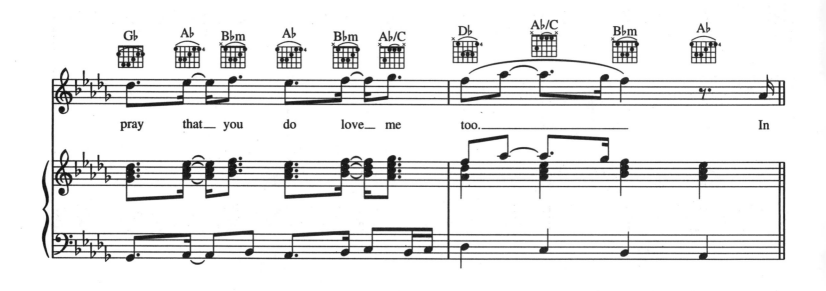

I thank God _____ that I fi-nal-ly found you. _____

All my life, _____ I pray for some-one _____ like you. Yes, I

pray that _____ you do love _____ me too. _____ In

Repeat ad lib. and fade

Verse 2:
Say, and I promise to never fall in love with a stranger.
You're all I'm thinkin', love, I praise the Lord above
For sendin' me your love, I cherish every hug.
I really love you so much.
(To Chorus:)

AMEN KIND OF LOVE

Words and Music by
TREY BRUCE and
WAYNE TESTER

Don't guess I've ever loved another. Never once before did I really see the light.

You've given love a brand new meaning, bound by a higher power than I've ever known before.

116

ANGEL OF MINE

Words and Music by
RHETT LAWRENCE and TRAVON POTTS

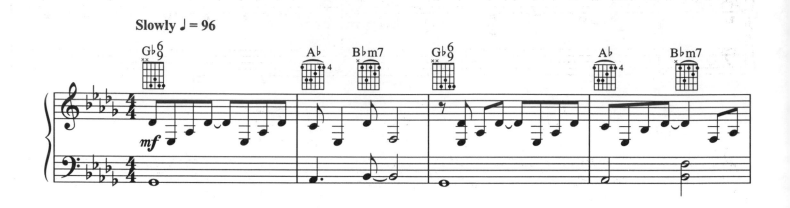

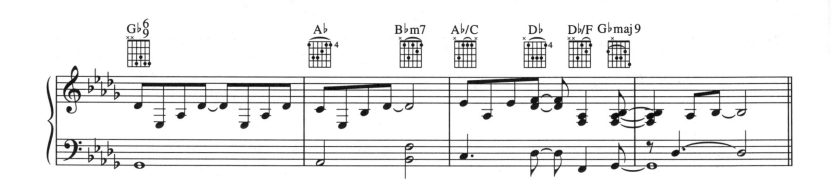

Verse 1:

1. When I first saw you, I al-read-y knew___ there was some-thing

Angel of Mine - 6 - 1

Verses 2 & 3:

2. I look at you look - ing at me____
3. Noth - ing means more to me than what we share.__

Now I know why they say the best things_ are free.____ I'm gon - na love you, boy, you
No one in this whole world can ev - er____ com - pare.____ Last night, the way you moved is

Pre-chorus 1 & 2:

1. How you changed my world, you'll nev-er know.__ I'm dif-f'rent now,___ you
2. What you mean to me, you'll nev-er know.__ Deep in-side___ I

Chorus:

helped me grow.__
need to show.__ } You came in-to my life straight from a-bove.__

When I lost all hope, you showed me love.__ I'm check-ing for you, boy, you're

Verse 5:

From the Twentieth Century Fox Motion Picture
"ANASTASIA"

AT THE BEGINNING

Lyrics by LYNN AHRENS

Music by STEPHEN FLAHERTY

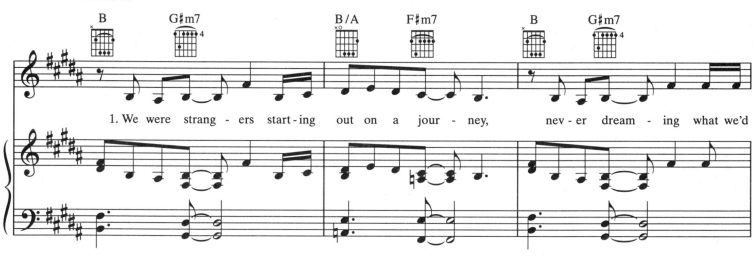

1. We were strang- ers start-ing out on a jour-ney, nev-er dream-ing what we'd

have to go through.___ Now here we are and I'm sud-den-ly stand-ing

At the Beginning - 7 - 1

AVE MARIA

FRANZ SCHUBERT, Op. 52

Ave Maria - 9 - 1

AVE MARIA

(From the First Prelude of Johann Sebastian Bach)

Adapted by CHARLES GOUNOD

From the M-G-M Musical Production "THE TOAST OF NEW ORLEANS"

BE MY LOVE

Lyric by
SAMMY CAHN

Music by
NICHOLAS BRODSZKY

Be My Love - 3 - 1

Be My Love - 3 - 2

146

Because You Love Me

Words and Music by
KOSTAS and JOHN SCOTT SHERRILL

Slowly ♩ = 60

(with pedal)

Verses 1 & 4:

1. I don't know_____ how I sur-vived_____ in this cold and emp-ty world for all___ this___
4. See additional lyrics

time. I on-ly know___ that I'm___ a-live___ be-cause___ you

love me.___ 2. When I___ re-

Because You Love Me - 3 - 1

Verse 3:
Instrumental solo ad lib.
(To Bridge:)

Verse 4:
I believe in things unseen;
I believe in the message of a dream.
And I believe in what you are
Because you love me.

Verse 5:
With all my heart
And all my soul,
I'm loving you and I never will let go.
And every day I let it show
Because you love me.
(To Coda)

BEST THING THAT EVER HAPPENED TO ME

Words and Music by
JIM WEATHERLY

151

Best Thing That Ever Happened to Me - 4 - 2

(THEY LONG TO BE)
CLOSE TO YOU

Words by
HAL DAVID

Music by
BURT BACHARACH

(They Long to Be) Close to You - 2 - 1

(They Long to Be) Close to You - 2 - 2

COULD I HAVE THIS DANCE

Words and Music by
WAYLAND HOLYFIELD and
BOB HOUSE

Moderately Slow

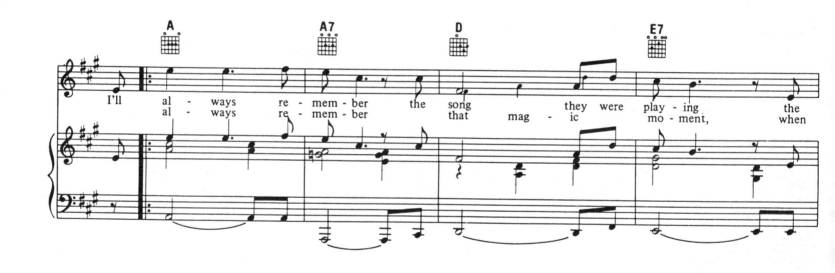

I'll al - ways re - mem - ber the song they were play - ing the
al - ways re - mem - ber that mag - ic mo - ment, when

first time_____ we danced and I knew.
I held_____ you close to me.

As we
As

Could I Have This Dance - 3 - 2

ENDLESS LOVE

Words and Music by
LIONEL RICHIE

EVERGREEN
Love Theme from "A Star Is Born"

Words by
PAUL WILLIAMS

Music by
BARBRA STREISAND

Evergreen - 6 - 1

FOREVER I DO
(The Wedding Song)

Words and Music by
CYNTHIA BIGGS and DEXTER WANSEL

FOREVER AND EVER, AMEN

Words and Music by DON SCHLITZ
and PAUL OVERSTREET

Forever and Ever, Amen - 7 - 1

THE HAWAIIAN WEDDING SONG
KE KALI NEI AU

English Words by
AL HOFFMAN and DICK MANNING
Hawaiian Words and Music
by CHARLES E. KING

*Symbols for Guitar, Diagrams for Ukulele.

The Hawaiian Wedding Song - 3 - 1

*Small notes for duet version with girl.

The Hawaiian Wedding Song - 3 - 2

The Hawaiian Wedding Song - 3 - 3

(I WANNA TAKE) FOREVER TONIGHT

Words and Music by
ANDY GOLDMARK
and ERIC CARMEN

is in your eyes.___ Whoa,_____ I wan - na take for -

ev - er___ to - night.___

2. Touch my lips,_ ev - er.___

Bridge:

And when I'm here be - side you, wan - na see what drives you out of your mind.___

HERE AND NOW

Words and Music by
TERRY STEELE and
DAVID ELLIOT

Here and Now - 4 - 1

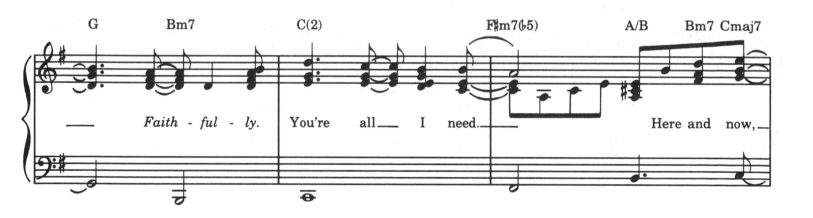

Here and Now - 4 - 2

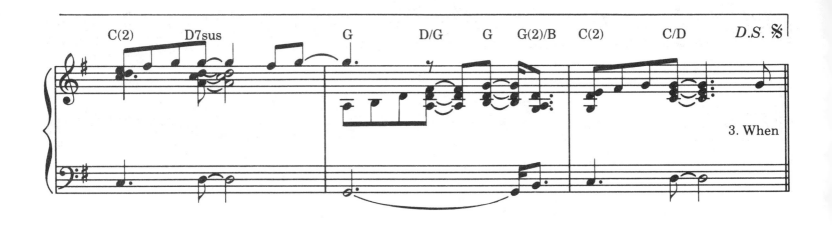

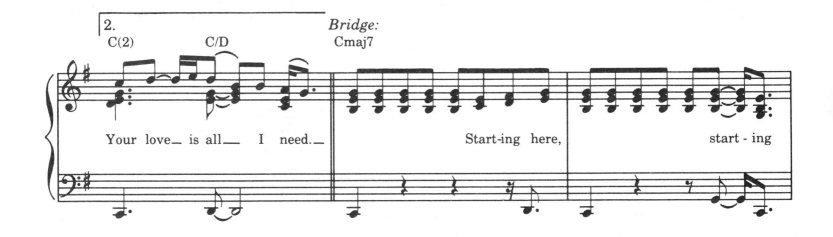

Verse 2:
I look in your eyes and there I see
What happiness really means.
The love that we share makes life so sweet,
Together we'll always be.
This pledge of love feels so right,
And ooh, I need you.
To Chorus:

Verse 3:
When I look in your eyes, there I see
All that a love should really be.
And I need you more and more each day,
Nothing can take your love away.
More than I dare to dream,
I need you.
To Chorus:

I BELIEVE IN YOU AND ME

Words and Music by
SANDY LINZER and DAVID WOLFERT

I Believe in You and Me - 4 - 1

Verse 2:
I will never leave your side,
I will never hurt your pride.
When all the chips are down,
I will always be around,
Just to be right where you are, my love.
Oh, I love you, boy.
I will never leave you out,
I will always let you in
To places no one has ever been.
Deep inside, can't you see?
I believe in you and me.
(To Bridge:)

I COULD NOT ASK FOR MORE

Words and Music by
DIANE WARREN

I DO

Words and Music by
PAUL BRANDT

Verse 3:
I know the time will disappear,
But this love we're building on will always be here.
No way that this is sinking sand,
On this solid rock we'll stand forever...
(To Chorus:)

I DO (CHERISH YOU)

Words and Music by
KEITH STEGALL and DAN HILL

*Enharmonic chord labeling of F♭maj7.

I Do (Cherish You) - 5 - 1

209

I Do (Cherish You) - 5 - 4

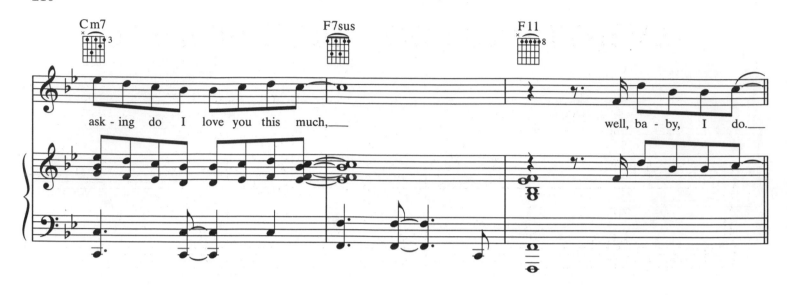

ask - ing do I love you this much,____ well, ba - by, I do.____

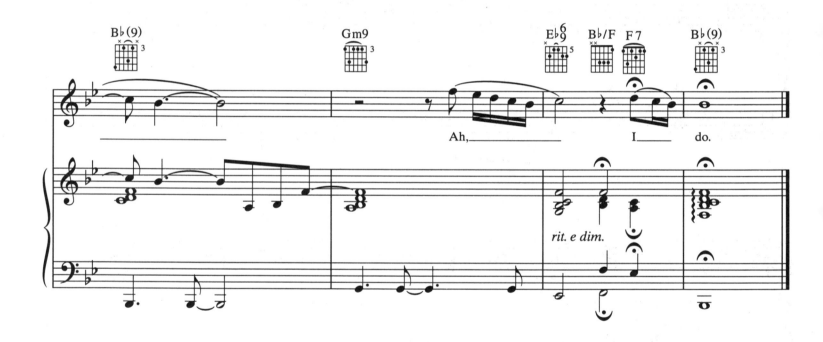

Ah,_____ I____ do.

rit. e dim.

Verse 2:
In my world before you,
I lived outside my emotions.
Didn't know where I was going
Till that day I found you.
How you opened my life
To a new paradise.
In a world torn by change,
Still with all of my heart,
Till my dying day . . .
(To Chorus:)

(EVERYTHING I DO) I DO IT FOR YOU

Written by
BRYAN ADAMS, ROBERT JOHN LANGE
and MICHAEL KAMEN

(Everything I Do) I Do It for You - 5 - 1

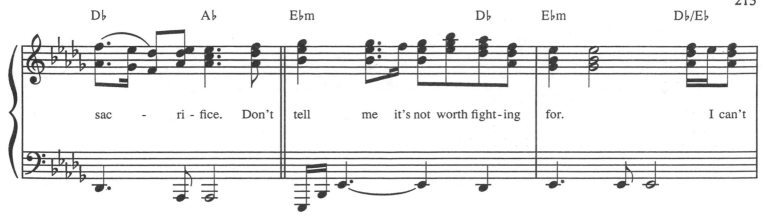

sac - ri - fice. Don't tell me it's not worth fight-ing for. I can't

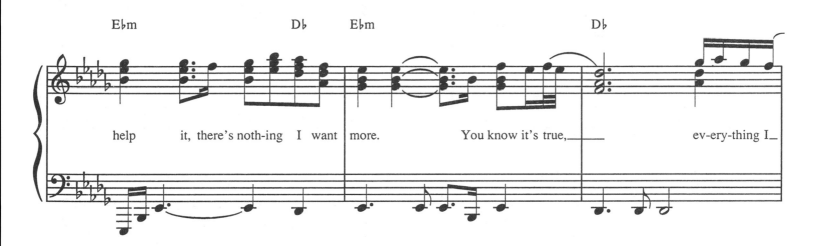

help it, there's noth-ing I want more. You know it's true,___ ev-ery-thing I___

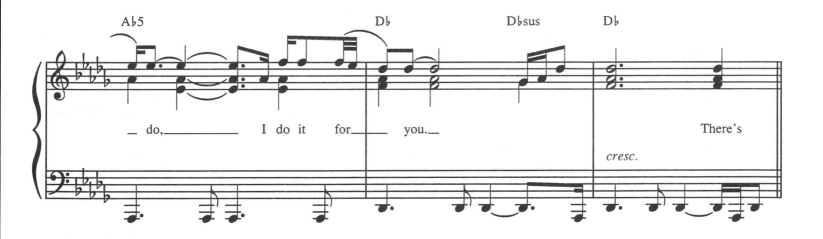

___ do,___ I do it for___ you.___ There's

no love___ like your love,___ and no___ oth - er could give

more___love. There's no - where_____ un-less you're_ there, all the

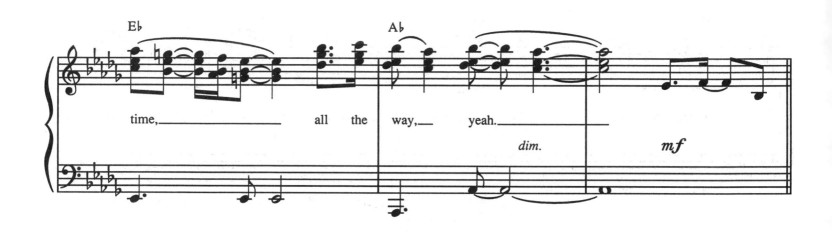

time,_____ all the way,___ yeah.___

dim. *mf*

(instrumental solo . . .

1.

2.

Oh, you can't tell me it's not worth try - in'

. . . end solo)

for.___ I can't help___ it, there's noth-ing I want more.___ Yeah,__ I would

cresc.　　　ƒ

fight__ for you,___ I'd lie___ for you,__ walk the wire___ for you,__ yeah,__ I'd

die for__ you.___ You know it's true, ev-'ry-thing I__

dim.　　mp

__do,___ oh,___ I do it for___ you.___

rit.　　　　dim.

I KNEW YOU WERE WAITING
(FOR ME)

Words and Music by
DENNIS MORGAN and
SIMON CLIMIE

I Knew You Were Waiting - 4 - 1

Verse 2:
With an endless desire, I kept on searchin', sure in time our eyes would meet.
Now like bridges on fire the hurt is over, one touch and you set me free.
I don't regret a single moment, oh, oh, lookin' back,
When I think of all those disappointments, I just laugh.
(To Chorus:)

IF THERE HADN'T BEEN YOU

Words and Music by
TOM SHAPIRO and RON SHELLARD

If There Hadn't Been You - 4 - 1

Verse 2:
A man filled with hope,
Who finally knows
Where he belongs.
A heart filled with love,
More than enough to keep it strong.
A life that's alive again,
No longer afraid to face the truth.
All of this I would have missed
If there hadn't been you.

IF YOU ASKED ME TO

Words and Music by
DIANE WARREN

Moderately slow ♩ = 84

Verse 1:

1. Used to be that I be-lieved in___ some-thing, used to be that I be-lieved in love._

It's been a long time since I've had that feel-ing: I could love some-one,___ I could

trust some-one.___ I said I'd nev-er let no-bod-y near my heart a-gain,___ dar-lin,'___

Verse 2:

IF YOU SAY MY EYES ARE BEAUTIFUL

Words and Music by
ELLIOT WILLENSKY

230

* cue size notes indicate vocal harmony

If You Say My Eyes Are Beautiful - 4 - 3

IN YOUR EYES

Words by
DAN HILL

Music by
MICHAEL MASSER

think I fi-n'lly know_you. I can see be-yond_your smile._ I
2. *(See additional lyrics)*

think that I_ can show_you_ that what we have_is still_worth-while._Don't you know that

love's just like the thread __ that keeps un - rav - el - ing, __ but then __ it

ties us back __ to-geth - er ___ in the _____ end?___ In your __

Chorus: eyes;

I can see __ my dream's re-flec - tions in your ___

eyes.

Found the an - swers to my ques-tions in your

Do   do do do _____   do do do do _____

_____   do   do   do   do   do   ooo   ooo   ooo.

dim. and poco rit.

mp

Verse 2:
But you warned me that life changes,
And that no one really knows
Whether time would make us strangers,
Or whether time would make us grow.
Even though the winds of time will change
In a world where nothing stays the same,
Through it all our love will still remain.

(To Chorus:)

THE IRISH WEDDING SONG

(The Wedding Song)

Words and Music by
IAN BETTERIDGE

The Irish Wedding Song - 3 - 1

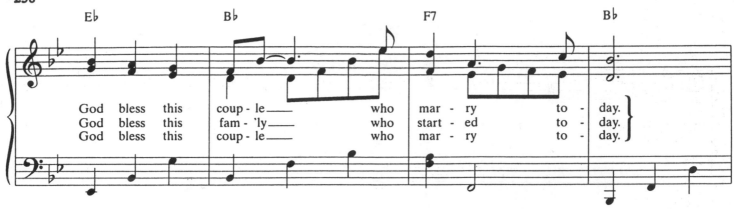

God bless this coup - le____ who mar - ry to - day.
God bless this fam - 'ly____ who start - ed to - day.
God bless this coup - le____ who mar - ry to - day.

Chorus

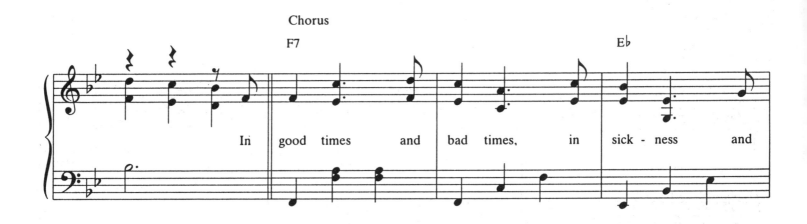

In good times and bad times, in sick - ness and

health,____ may they know that rich - es are not need - ed for

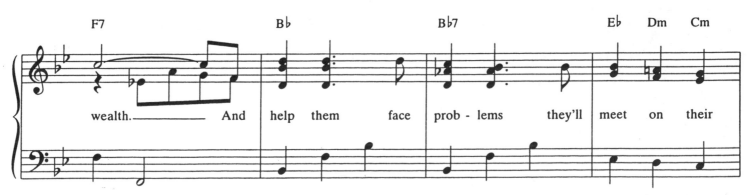

wealth._____ And help them face prob - lems they'll meet on their

The Irish Wedding Song - 3 - 2

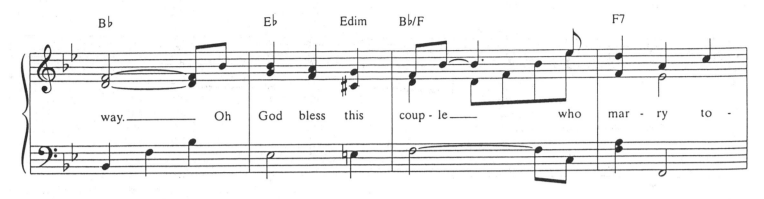

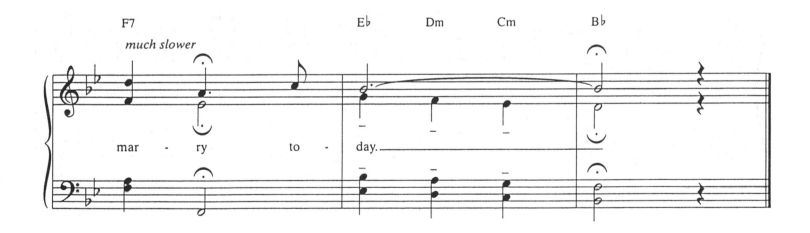

The Irish Wedding Song - 3 - 3

INSEPARABLE

Words and Music by
CHARLES JACKSON and
MARVIN JEROME YANCY

Inseparable - 4 - 1

I'LL STILL LOVE YOU MORE

Words and Music by
DIANE WARREN

1. Ask me how much____ you mean to me,_____ and I would-n't
2. *See additional lyrics*

e - ven____ know____ where to____ start.____ Ask if this love____ runs

deep in me;_____ you won't find a deep - er____ love____ in an - y heart.

I'll Still Love You More - 4 - 1

Verse 2:
Ask me just what I'd do for you;
I'll tell you that I would do anything.
Ask if this heart beats true for you;
I'll show you a truer heart could never be.
You could say there's not a star that you won't bring me.
You could say there'll be no day that you won't need me.
You could think no other love could last as long,
But you'd be wrong,
You'd be wrong.
(To Chorus:)

I'VE DREAMED OF YOU

Words and Music by
ANN HAMPTON CALLAWAY
and ROLF LOVLAND

I've Dreamed of You - 5 - 1

And all my life I have searched for you ev - 'ry -
That first look in your eyes, I can't for -

where.
get.

I caught your smile in the
You melt - ed me with your

morn - ing sun, I heard your whis - per on the breeze at night. I
ten - der touch. I felt all fear and sor - row slip a - way. Now,

prayed one day that your arms would hold me tight.
here we stand, hand in hand, this bless - ed

I've Dreamed of You - 5 - 2

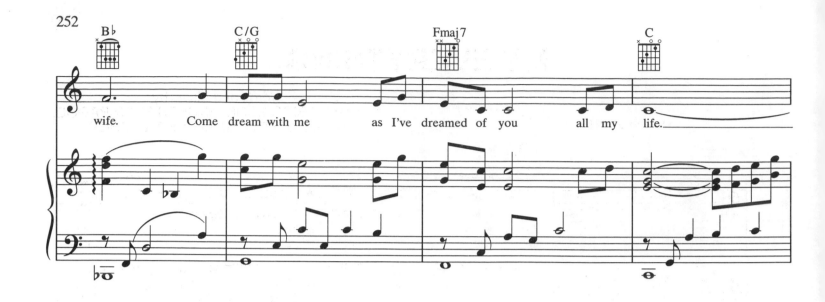

wife.   Come dream with me   as I've dreamed of you   all my   life.____

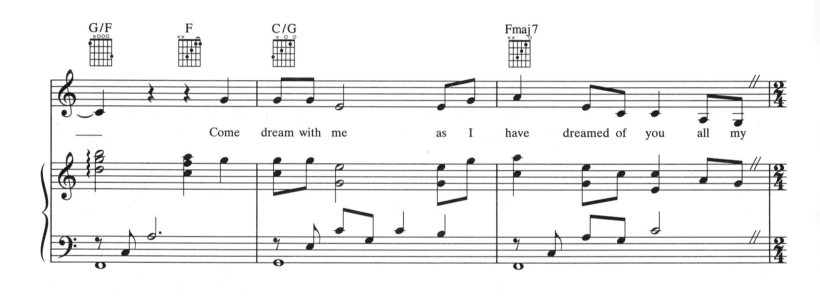

____   Come   dream with me   as I   have   dreamed of you   all my

life.____

MY EVERYTHING

Words and Music by
ARNTHOR BIRGISSON, ANDERS SVEN BAGGE,
NICK LACHEY and ANDREW LACHEY

Slowly ♩ = 64

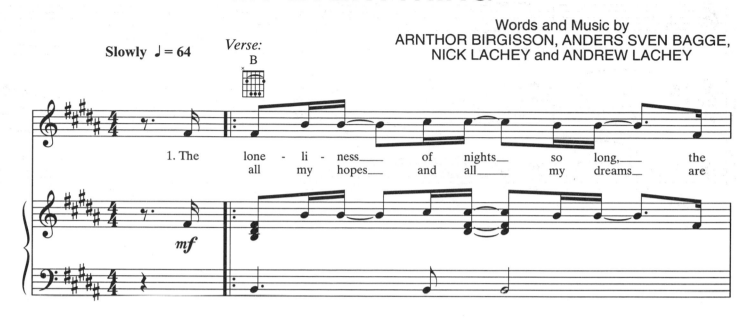

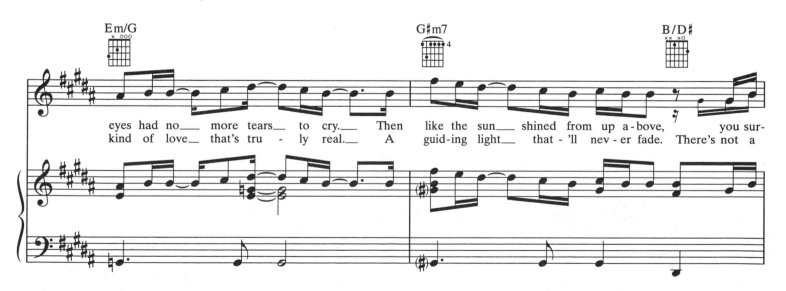

My Everything - 5 - 1

1. Dm7 ... B♭maj7 ... Dm7/G

night I pray___ on bend - ed knee___ that you will al - ways be___ You are my my ev - e - ry -

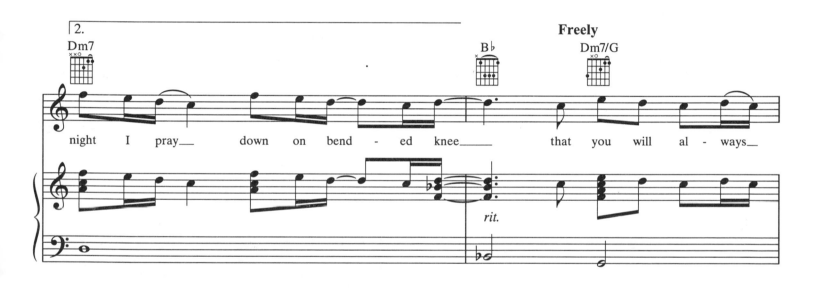

2. Dm7 ... **Freely** ... B♭ Dm7/G

night I pray___ down on bend - ed knee_____ that you will al - ways___

rit.

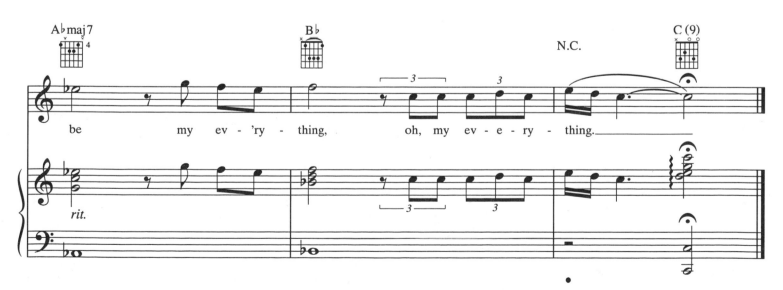

A♭maj7 ... B♭ ... N.C. ... C (9)

be my ev - 'ry - thing, oh, my ev - e - ry - thing._____

rit.

THE KEEPER OF THE STARS

Words and Music by
DICKEY LEE, DANNY MAYO
and KAREN STALEY

He sure knew what he___ was do - in'___ when he joined these two___

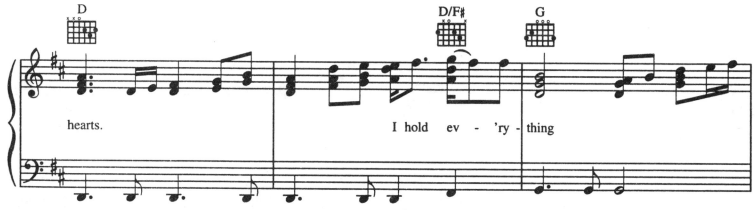

hearts. I hold ev - 'ry - thing

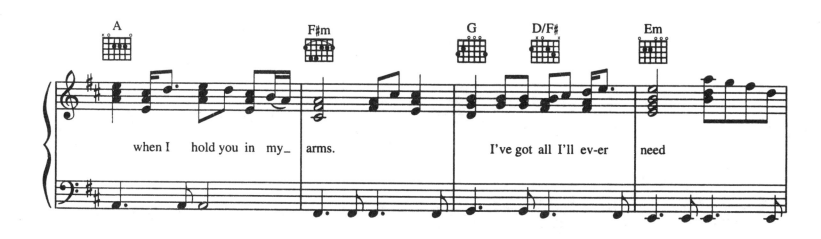

when I hold you in my___ arms. I've got all I'll ev-er need

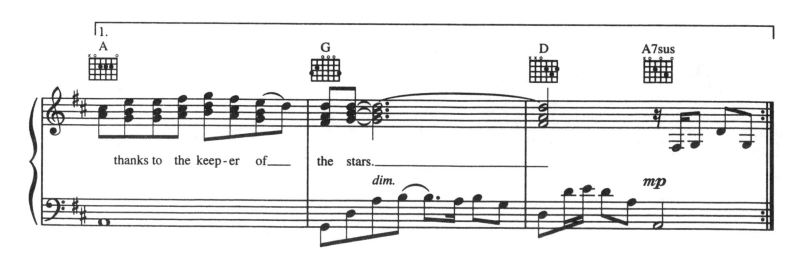

1.

thanks to the keep-er of___ the stars.___

dim.

mp

LOVE LIKE OURS

Lyrics by
ALAN and MARILYN BERGMAN

Music by
DAVE GRUSIN

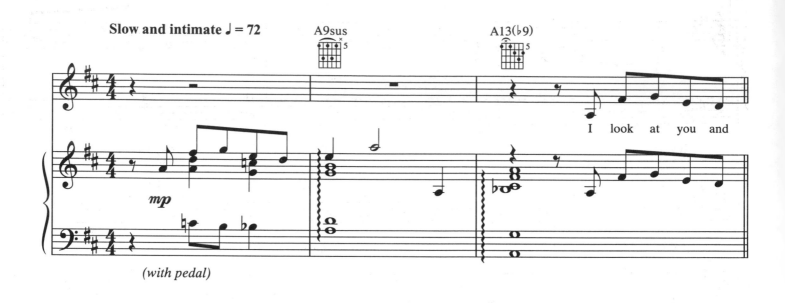

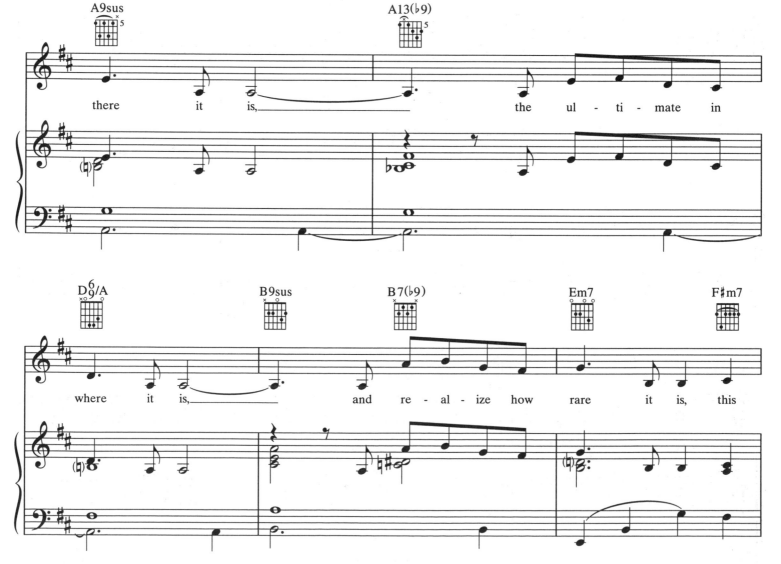

Love Like Ours - 4 - 1

From the Motion Picture "LOVE STORY"

LOVE STORY (Where Do I Begin)

Lyric by
CARL SIGMAN

Music by
FRANCIS LAI

Where Do I Be-gin to tell the sto-ry of how great a love can be,
With her first hel-lo she gave a mean-ing to this emp-ty world of mine;

The sweet love sto-ry that is old-er than the sea, The sim-ple truth a-bout the
There'd nev-er be an-oth-er love, an-oth-er time; She came in-to my life and

love she brings to me? Where do I start?
made the liv-ing fine.

Love Story (Where Do I Begin) - 3 - 1

Love Story (Where Do I Begin) - 3 - 3

ONE HEART ONE LOVE

Words and Music by
GARY BROWN and BARRY EASTMOND

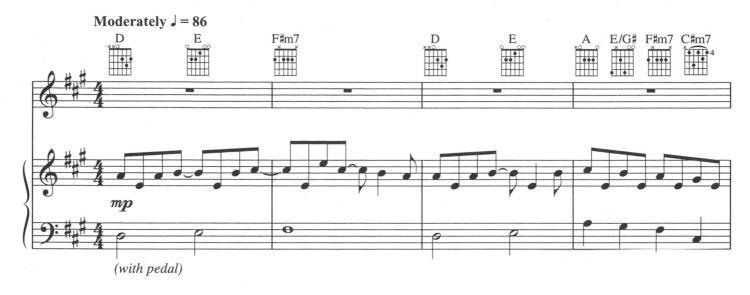

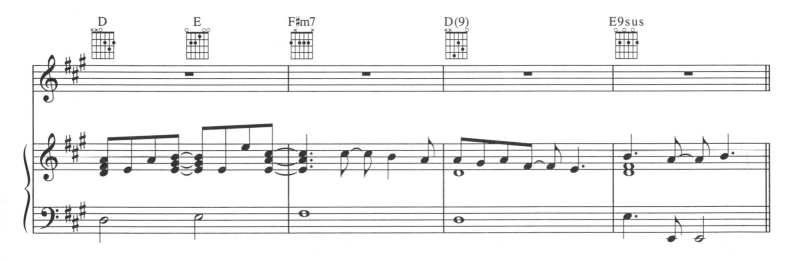

Verse:

1. I'm put-tin' my heart in your hands.
2. You showed your trust in my heart.

One Heart One Love - 5 - 1

Chorus:

One heart,___ one love,___ one love now, ba - by. I'm giv-ing my all to you___ now, ba - by.___ One heart,___ one love.___ For the rest of my days___ I prom - ise that I'll___ be true.

prom - ise that I'll___ be true___ to you.

MY OWN TRUE LOVE
Based on "Tara Theme"

Words by
MACK DAVID

Music by
MAX STEINER

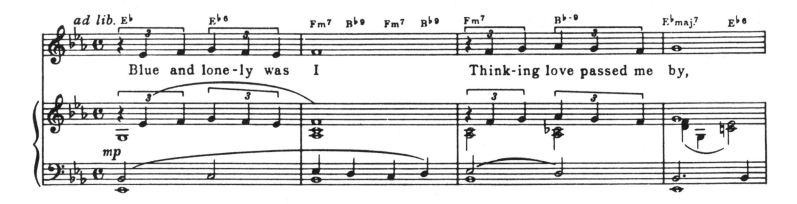

Blue and lone-ly was I Think-ing love passed me by,

All at once all my grey days Turned in-to gay days And I know why:

REFRAIN–Slowly

MY OWN TRUE LOVE, MY OWN TRUE LOVE, At last I've found you,

My Own True Love - 2 - 1

NOW AND FOREVER

Words and Music by
RICHARD MARX

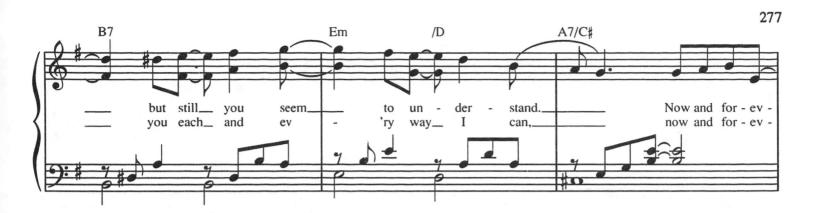

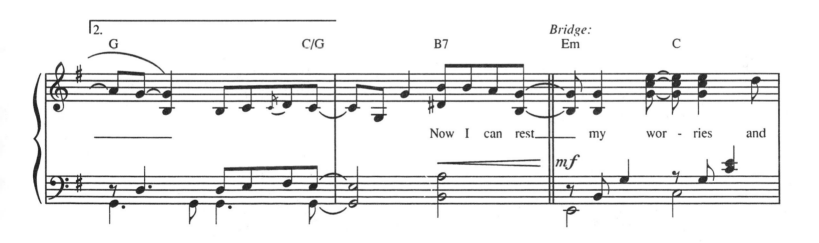

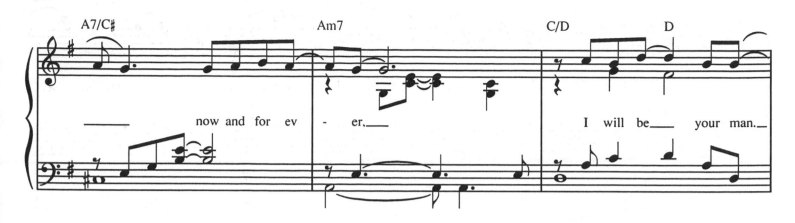

now and for ev - er,_____ I will be_____ your man._____

_____ Now and for - ev - er,

I will be_____ your man.

poco rit. e dim.

mp

OH PROMISE ME!

Words by
CLEMENT SCOTT

Music by
REGINALD DE KOVEN
OP. 50

Oh Prom-ise Me that some day you and I will take our love to-geth-er to some sky Where we can be a-lone, and faith re-new, And find the hol-lows where those flow-ers grew, Those first sweet vi-o-lets of ear-ly spring, Which come in whis-pers, thrill us both, and sing of love un-speak-a-ble that is to be; Oh Prom-ise Me! Oh Prom-ise Me!

Oh Promise Me! - 2 - 1

ONCE IN A LIFETIME

Words and Music by
WALTER AFANASIEFF, MICHAEL BOLTON
and DIANE WARREN

Lyrics:

1. Some peo-ple fill__ their lives__ with emp-ty nights__ and days__ that slip a-way.__
2. Some peo-ple live__ their lives__ in com-pro-mise__ and hide__ their dreams a-way.__

Once in a Lifetime - 6 - 1

PRECIOUS THING

Words and Music by
STEVE WARINER and
MAC McANALLY

Chorus:

Precious Thing - 3 - 1

Verse 2:
(Inst. solo ad lib.)

Verse 3:
If our bills are paid on time,
Or if we let 'em get way behind,
I still feel like you and me
Are just sittin' on a goldmine.
What more could I ask for.
Honey I'll never be poor,
'Cause I own the world,
As long as you're here by my side.
(To Chorus:)

SAVING FOREVER FOR YOU

Words and Music by
DIANE WARREN

SO IN LOVE WITH YOU

Words and Music by
LINDA THOMPSON, DAVID FOSTER
and BILL ROSS

Slowly ♩ = 69

1. You are to me___ what po-e-try___ tries to say_ with a word.___
2. *See additional lyrics*

You are the song,___ all the mu-sic___ my heart_ ev-er heard.

I can't es-cape;_ the air___that I breathe e-ven speaks of you___ and

So in Love With You - 4 - 1

Verse 2:
Words can't express what I confess with each beat of my heart,
I'm overwhelmed with the passion I felt from the start.
Our love will grow as the years come and go
I'll remain by your side, oh yes I will.
There isn't anything that I would deny.
(To Chorus:)

TAKING YOU HOME

Words and Music by
DON HENLEY,
STAN LYNCH and STUART BRAWLEY

302

Taking You Home - 6 - 3

Tak - ing___ you home.

home.

Verse 3:
There were days, lonely days
When the world wouldn't throw me a crumb.
But I kept on believing that this day would come.
(*To Chorus:*)

Verse 4:
(*Instrumental solo ad lib.*)
(*To Chorus:*)

From the Columbia Motion Picture "ICE CASTLES"

THEME FROM ICE CASTLES

Lyrics by CAROLE BAYER SAGER (Through the Eyes of Love) Music by MARVIN HAMLISCH

Please, don't let this feel - ing
now I can take the
Please, don't let this feel - ing

end. It's ev-'ry-thing I am, ev-'ry-thing I want to be.
time. I can see my life as it comes up shin - ing now.
end. It might not come a - gain and I want to re - mem - ber

Theme From Ice Castles - 3 - 1

now   I   do   be-lieve   that   e-ven   in   the   storm   we'll   find _____ some

light.   Know-ing   you're   be-side   me   I'm   all __ right. _____

D.S. al Coda

Coda

through   the   eyes _____ of   love.

Theme From Ice Castles - 3 - 3

TO ME

Slowly and expressively ♩ = 69

Words and Music by
MACK DAVID and
MIKE REED

Verse:

To me, you are the hand that I reach for
me, you are the truth I be-lieve in;

when I've lost my way. To me, you are the
I be-lieve in you. To me, you are the

first star of eve-ning, the sun that warms my day.
love I have looked for my whole life through.

Just as

To Me - 3 - 1

YOU'RE THE INSPIRATION

Words and Music by
PETER CETERA and
DAVID FOSTER

314

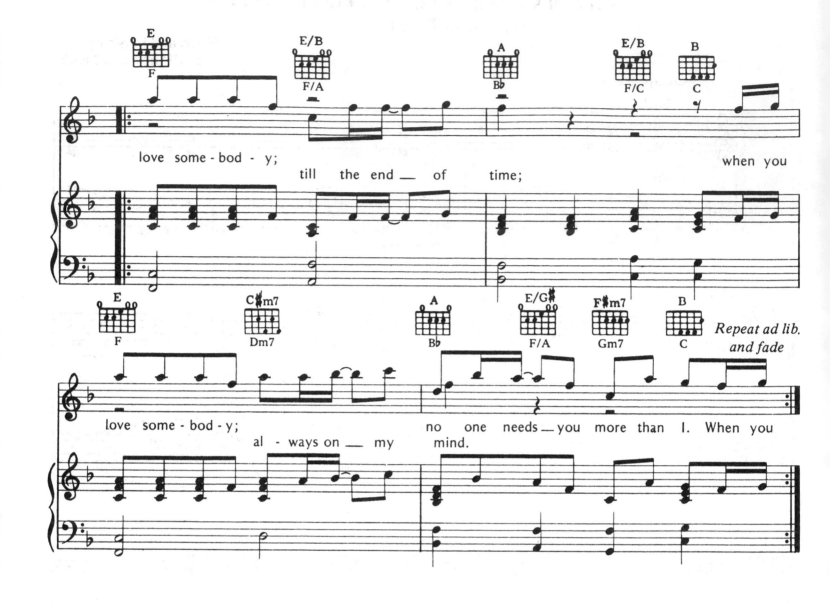

𝄋 *Verse 2:*

And I know (yes, I know)
That it's plain to see
We're so in love when we're together.
Now I know (now I know)
That I need you here with me
From tonight until the end of time.
You should know everywhere I go;
Always on my mind, you're in my heart, in my soul.

(To Chorus:)

THE VOWS GO UNBROKEN
(Always True to You)

Words and Music by
GARY BURR and ERIC KAZ

The Vows Go Unbroken - 3 - 1

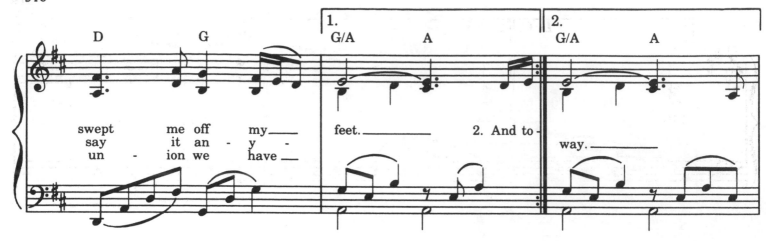

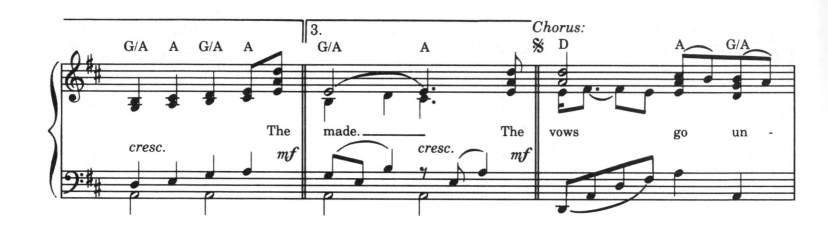

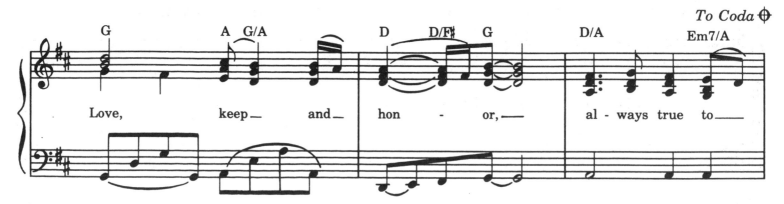

The Vows Go Unbroken - 3 - 2

TWO HEARTS

Words and Music by
BOB PARR

Verse 2:
Were there times you thought you had no more to give me?
Were there times you thought you had to walk away?
Did you see me standing there?
Did the feeling catch you unaware,
Remembering the good times that we shared?
Ooh, when I face eternity,
Or the love that set my heart free,
I'll never turn away, I know you're here to stay.
(To Chorus:)

Two Hearts - 4 - 4

From the Motion Picture "AN OFFICER AND A GENTLEMAN"

UP WHERE WE BELONG

Words by
WILL JENNINGS

Music by
BUFFY SAINTE-MARIE
and JACK NITZSCHE

Up Where We Belong - 4 - 1

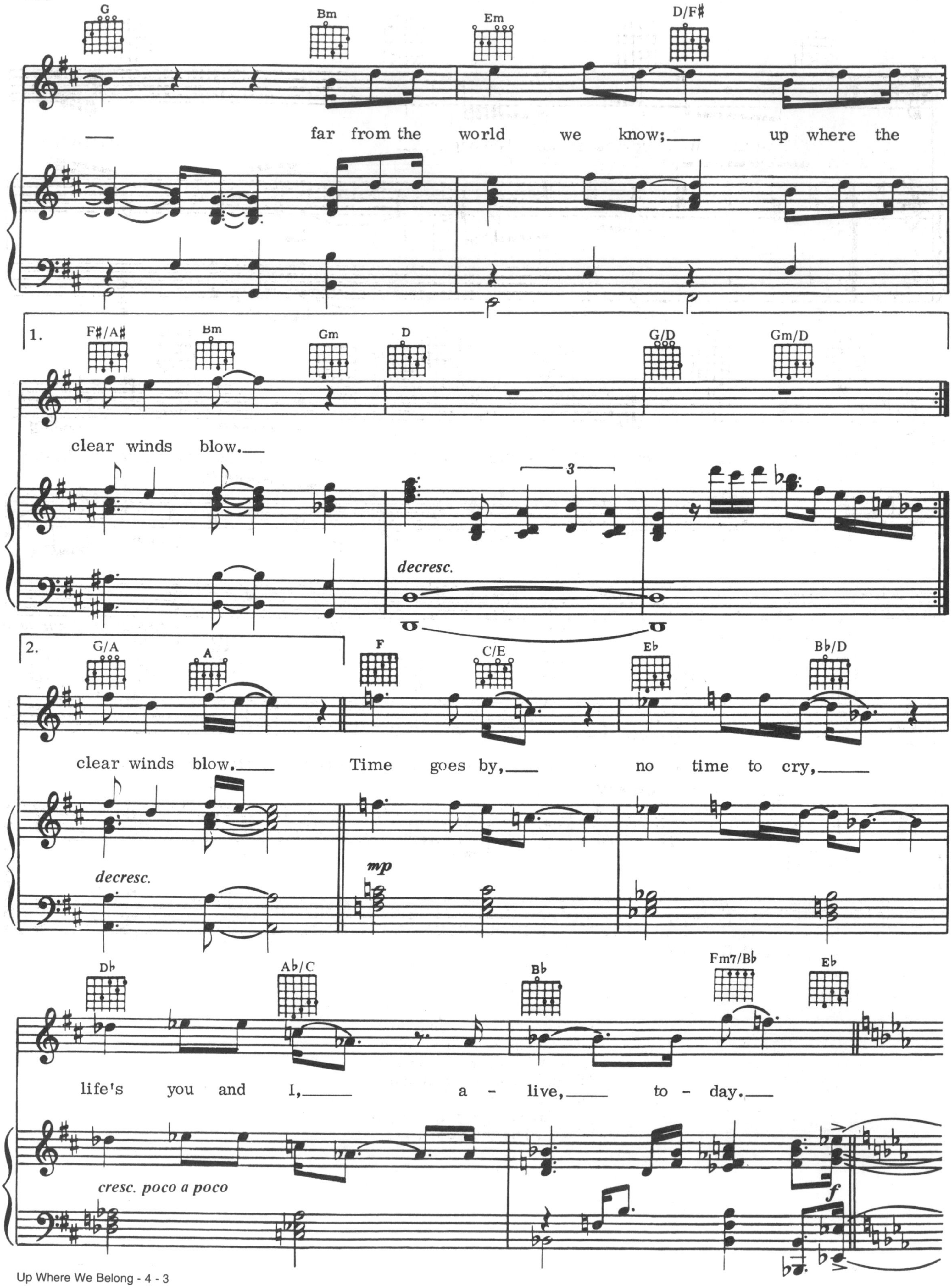

G
Bm
Em
D/F♯
far from the world we know; up where the
1.
F♯/A♯
Bm
Gm
D
G/D
Gm/D
clear winds blow.
3
decresc.
2.
G/A
A
F
C/E
E♭
B♭/D
clear winds blow. Time goes by, no time to cry,
decresc.
mp
D♭
A♭/C
B♭
Fm7/B♭
E♭
life's you and I, a - live, to - day.
cresc. poco a poco
f

Verse 2:
Some hang on to "used-to-be",
Live their lives looking behind.
All we have is here and now;
All our life, out there to find.
The road is long.
There are mountains in our way,
But we climb them a step every day.

VALENTINE

Composed by
JIM BRICKMAN and JACK KUGELL

Moderately ♩ = 92

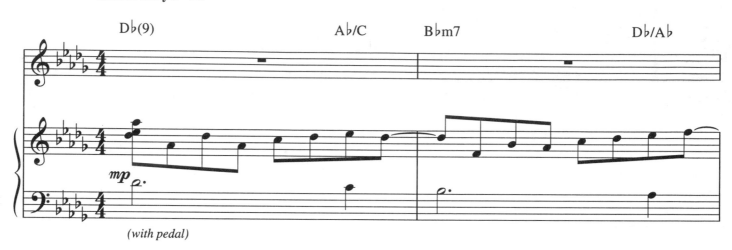

If there were no words,____ no way to speak,____ I

Valentine - 6 - 1

Valentine - 6 - 4

THE WEDDING MARCH
(From "Midsummer Night's Dream")

Music by
FELIX MENDELSSOHN

Allegro

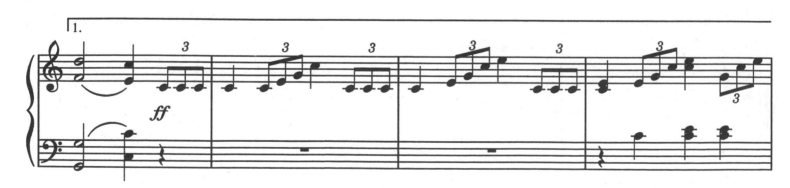

The Wedding March - 2 - 1

WHAT A DIFFERENCE
YOU'VE MADE IN MY LIFE

Words and Music by ARCHIE JORDAN

What a dif - 'frence you've made _ in my life; _____ what a dif - 'frence you've made _ in my life. _____
change you have made _ in my heart; _____ what a change you have made _ in my heart. _____

You're my sun - shine day _ and night. _____ Oh what a
You re - placed all the bro - ken parts. _____ Oh what a

dif - 'frence you've made _____ in my life. _____
change you have made _____ in my

What a Difference You've Made in My Life - 4 - 1

What a Difference You've Made in My Life - 4 - 4

YOUR LOVE AMAZES ME

Words and Music by
CHUCK JONES and AMANDA HUNT

Verse 2:
I've seen a sunset that would make you cry,
And colors of a rainbow reaching 'cross the sky.
The moon in all its phases, but
Your love amazes me.
To Chorus:

Verse 3:
I've prayed for miracles that never came.
I got down on my knees in the pouring rain.
But only you could save me,
Your love amazes me.
(To Chorus:)

YEARS FROM HERE

Words and Music by
GARY BAKER, JERRY WILLIAMS
and FRANK J. MYERS

Verse:

1. Stand - ing here face to face,_____ I feel my heart
2. I can prom - ise you this_____ with ev - 'ry breath

_____ o - ver - flow - ing with love and e - mo - tion. The mo - ment you took my hand,_____
_____ I take,_____ I'll live to love____ you. I'll go a - bove and be - yond____

_____ there was no doubt____ in my mind___ a - bout our fu - ture.
_____ to give you ev - 'ry - thing___ that one man can give____ you.

Years From Here - 3 - 1

YOU ARE THE LOVE OF MY LIFE

Words and Music by
MICHAEL MASSER and LINDA CREED

Slowly and expressively ♩ = 63

You Are the Love of My Life - 3 - 1

CUTTING THE CAKE
(The Farmer in the Dell)

TRADITIONAL
Arranged by PAMELA SCHULTZ

bride cuts the cake. _____ The bride cuts the cake.

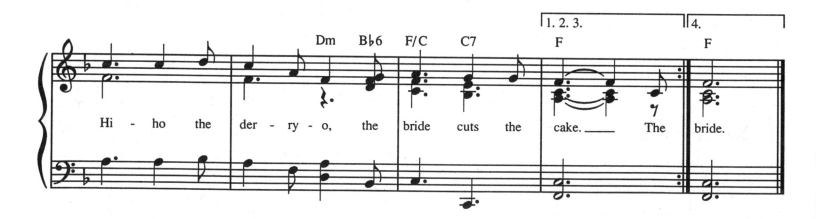

Hi - ho the der - ry - o, the bride cuts the cake. _____ The bride.

Verse 2:
The groom cuts the cake.
The groom cuts the cake.
Hi-ho the derry-o,
The groom cuts the cake.

Verse 3:
The bride feeds the groom.
The bride feeds the groom.
Hi-ho the derry-o,
The bride feeds the groom.

Verse 4:
The groom feeds the bride.
The groom feeds the bride.
Hi-ho the derry-o,
The groom feeds the bride.

TRUE LOVE

Words and Music by
COLE PORTER

True Love - 3 - 1

TRULY

Words and Music by
LIONEL RICHIE

Truly - 3 - 1